AN OFFICIAL WHOHQ BOOK

Who Was?
WORKBOOK
SUMMER ACTIVITIES

Based on the #1 *New York Times* Best-Selling Who Was? Series

Reading passages with comprehension, vocabulary, and writing activities, plus puzzles, mazes, and tons of fun!

written by Catherine Nichols

PENGUIN WORKSHOP
An imprint of Penguin Random House LLC, New York

First published in the United States of America by Penguin Workshop, an imprint of
Penguin Random House LLC, New York, 2022

Cover illustration by Nancy Harrison
Interior illustrations by Nancy Harrison, Mattia Cerato, Tim Haggerty, Gary LaCoste,
Scott MacNeill, Barbara Schaffer, and Chris Vallo

Visit us online at penguinrandomhouse.com.

Printed in the United States of America

ISBN 9780593225783   10 9 8 7 6 5 4 3 2 1 COMM

Designed by Dinardo Design

Who Was?
WORKBOOK

What's Inside?

Welcome to the wonderful world of Who Was?, full of history and the famous people who made it memorable. This summer workbook is packed with fascinating fact-filled passages about people you'll want to read about throughout the summer. It also has fun activities that will help you become a better reader and writer. Here's what you'll find:

Just for Fun! pages contain crossword puzzles, word searches, connect-the-dot puzzles, mazes, and more!

Read and Annotate pages are loaded with interesting facts about famous people. Mark up the passages as you read to help you better remember the facts. You can circle, underline, draw, and add notes.

Digging Deeper pages show how much you learned. So, show off!

Word Play pages help you have fun with new words and word parts. You'll want to impress your friends and family!

The Write Stuff pages give you space to be creative and connect what you read to your life.

A-Mazing Soccer

Pelé is a world-famous soccer player from Brazil. He is known for his amazing kicks and goals. Help Pelé kick the soccer ball to the goal.

START

FINISH

Finger Puppet

The Muppets are famous puppets. But who made them? A man named Jim Henson did. His first Muppet was Kermit the Frog. Jim made Kermit out of an old coat, some cardboard, felt, and a Ping-Pong ball.

Make your own puppet. Just follow the steps below.

1 Get a square sheet of paper. Fold the bottom third up.

2 Fold over the other side. If you want, you can tape it. Now you have a tube.

3 To make the puppet's head, fold the top down.

4 Give your puppet a face.

5 Put your puppet on your finger and have fun!

My puppet's name is

_____

A Great Sprinter
Jesse Owens

As you read:

- Underline important words
- Circle confusing words or sentences
- Add drawings or notes to remember important facts

NOTES

_____

_____

_____

_____

_____

_____

_____

_____

_____

Jesse Owens started running when he was just a young boy living in Alabama. And he never stopped.

He sprinted across farmland his family rented. He ran along dirt roads. He ran to the fields where he helped pick cotton. He ran to the orchards. He ran with friends, too. Jesse ran because it made him feel free. "I always loved running," he later said.

"Jesse would run and play just like everyone else," his cousin said. "But you could never catch him." No one ever did catch Jesse Owens. He became one of the greatest sprinters in history.

In 1936, Jesse competed in the Summer

Olympic Games. The games were held in Germany that year. On August 3, he was in the final race for the 100-meter dash. He approached the starting line. Next to him were runners from the Netherlands, Germany, and Sweden. There were two fellow Americans, too.

The crowd grew silent. They were waiting for the starting pistol. *Crack!* At the sound, Jesse and the other runners sprinted forward. The race was close for only a moment. Then Jesse pulled ahead. He sprinted across the finish line first. He was a gold-medal champion! Jesse went on to win three more gold medals. He became a hero all around the world.

NOTES

Big News!

Jesse Owens won four Olympic gold medals. Reporters all over the world wrote about this important story. Imagine you were one of these reporters. Write your story about Jesse Owens in the space below. Make sure to answer the questions in the box.

Who is your report about?

When did it take place?

Where did it take place?

What happened?

The Sports Page

By _____

_____

_____

_____

_____

_____

_____

_____

Shades of Meaning

Jesse Owens liked to **run**. He would **sprint** across farmland.
The words *run* and *sprint* have almost the same meaning.
But they are different. You could run at any speed.
But if you sprint, you are running fast.

Put each word from the word bank where it belongs
on the chart below.

Word Bank

Hop	Messy	Leap	Freezing	Pop
Race	Jog	Filthy	Explode	Chilly

Run	Cold	Dirty	Burst	Jump

On the Move
Laura Ingalls Wilder

As you read:

- Underline important words
- Circle confusing words or sentences
- Add drawings or notes to remember important facts

NOTES

_____

_____

_____

_____

_____

_____

_____

_____

_____

In 1874, two horses pulled a covered wagon. They were going across the prairie. A man held the horses' reins. Inside the wagon were the man's wife and daughters. One daughter was named Laura. She was seven years old. Laura looked out the back of the wagon. The prairie stretched to the skyline. Not a tree was in sight.

The family was traveling west. They were going to a new home. To Laura, this trip meant adventure. At night, the family camped outside. Pa played his fiddle. Laura looked up at the dark sky. She thought that "the stars were singing."

The family would enjoy many happy times like this. But they faced terrible times, too. Everything about frontier life was hard. In winter, there were blizzards. In summer, the land was as dry as dust. There was sickness and the danger of wild animals.

Laura grew up and married. But she always remembered the adventures of her childhood. Later, she wrote a book for children about these adventures. It was called *Little House in the Big Woods*. Laura kept writing. She wrote many more books about her childhood. Laura Ingalls Wilder became one of the best-loved children's authors ever.

NOTES

Simile Match-Up

A simile compares one thing to another. Here are some examples:

In summer, the land was dry as dust.
The girl's hair shone like a new penny.

Match the similes.

As fast as

As slow as

As big as

As cold as

As hard as

As sharp as

As quiet as

Write a simile that describes you.

I am as _____ as _____.

My Home

Laura's first book was called *Little House in the Big Woods*. Think about your home. Write a memory that happened there.

Draw a picture of your home.

Candy Man
Milton Hershey

As you read:

- Underline important words
- Circle confusing words or sentences
- Add drawings or notes to remember important facts

NOTES

_____

_____

_____

_____

_____

_____

_____

_____

_____

It is the year 1900. You are in an American candy store. The store looks very different than a store today. Back then, candy was a special treat. It was sold mostly in candy stores. Customers didn't touch the candy. It didn't come in wrappers and bars. It wasn't set out on open racks. It was kept in glass jars behind a counter. Shop clerks put candy into bags.

There was plenty of candy to choose from. Customers could buy butterscotch and taffy. They could buy molasses candy, toffee, and caramel. But Milton Hershey knew the one thing that was missing: chocolate. At that time, very few Americans had ever tasted milk chocolate. Milton Hershey had tried it in Europe. Hershey was a successful caramel maker. He thought milk chocolate was much better than any other candy. He thought it was better than his own caramels!

Hershey worked hard to bring milk chocolate to America. After many years, he succeeded. The Hershey chocolate bar changed the way Americans enjoyed candy. They could afford it. They could carry it with them. Each bar was wrapped. The bar was sold in drugstores and grocery stores. Best of all, the Hershey chocolate bar made chocolate available to everyone.

Candy Stores Then and Now

Compare a candy store in the year 1900 to a candy store today.
How are they different? How are they the same?

Candy Store in 1900	**Candy Store Today**

My Candy Store

Milton Hershey was a candy maker. He also owned candy stores. Imagine you had your own candy store.

What is the name of your store? _____

Where is your store? _____

When is your store open? _____

What candy is on the shelves? _____

What do you do in your store? _____

_____

_____

_____

Draw a picture of your store.

Hidden Chimps

Jane Goodall is a scientist who went to Africa to study wild chimps. Where are they? Find and circle all the chimps hiding in the picture.

Jane Goodall

How many chimps did you find? _____

A Dream Come True
Roberto Clemente

As you read:

- Underline important words
- Circle confusing words or sentences
- Add drawings or notes to remember important facts

NOTES

_____

_____

_____

_____

_____

_____

_____

_____

_____

I t was a sunny autumn day in Puerto Rico in 1952. Roberto Clemente arrived at a ball field. He was 18 years old. He was wearing beat-up baseball pants. He was carrying his old glove. He wore a cap with a long bill.

The field was mostly dirt. The baseballs there were used and scuffed. But that didn't matter to Roberto. He had showed up at the field for a major-league tryout. So had 70 or so other young players. All of them had the same goal. They wanted to be discovered by a scout from a Major League Baseball team. A scout is a person who looks for promising new players. For Roberto, making the majors would be a dream come true.

Roberto did his best to impress the scouts. He fired perfect throws from the outfield. He whizzed around the bases. He ran a 60-yard dash in 6.4 seconds. And he hit the ball hard, time after time. After watching Roberto, the scouts agreed. He had the skills to join the major leagues.

A year later, his major league dream came true. Roberto Clemente signed with the Brooklyn Dodgers. He went on to have one of baseball's most impressive careers.

NOTES

Baseball Talk

Look at the word in each baseball.
Write a fact from the passage using each word.

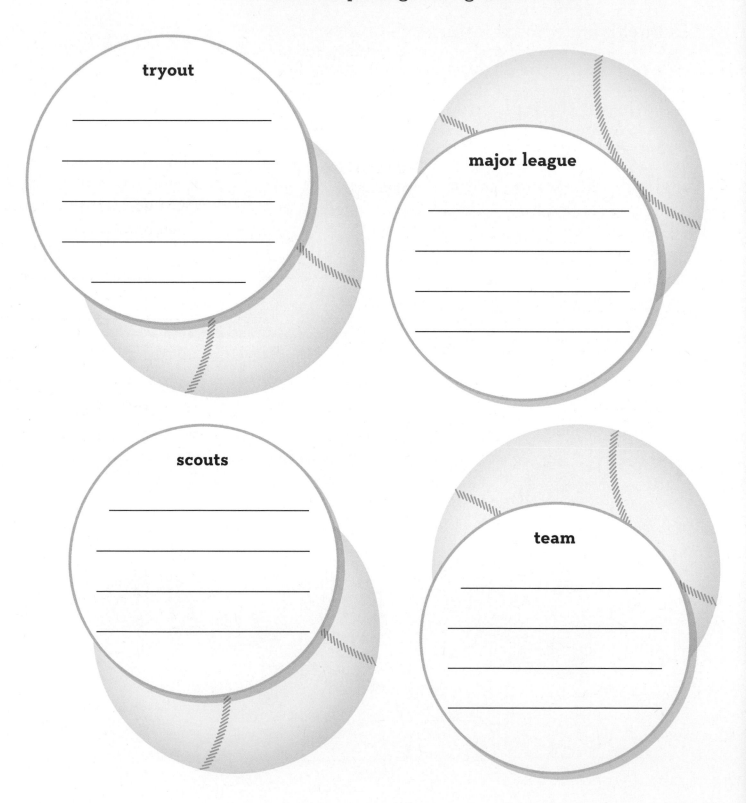

tryout

_____
_____
_____
_____
_____

major league

_____
_____
_____
_____

scouts

_____
_____
_____

team

_____
_____
_____

Around the Bases

Answer each question to get around the bases.
Can you score a home run?

How fast did Roberto Clemente
run the 60-yard dash?

_____

Second Base

What was Roberto
Clemente's goal?

_____

_____

_____

First Base

Which team did Roberto
Clemente sign with?

_____

_____

Third Base

Home Plate

When was the tryout held?

_____

_____

An Important Battle
George Washington

NOTES

America's War of Independence lasted from 1775 to 1783. Everyone knows how it ended. The colonists won. But they weren't expected to! The British army was mighty. It was the best-trained fighting machine in the world. It seemed as if the colonists had little chance against England.

George Washington was the leader of the Continental Army. By 1781, the Continental Army was not doing well. But one battle changed everything.

The leader of the British army had moved his men to Yorktown, Virginia. Yorktown was on a peninsula. It was surrounded on three sides by water.

American ships headed into the area. Then Washington sent in more soldiers. They gathered at the peninsula's tip. Washington now had 21,000 men ready to fight. The British only had about 7,000. The British army was outnumbered. It was also surrounded on all sides. The British were trapped!

The battle began. It lasted eight days. On October 17, 1781, the leader of the British army surrendered. Washington's big victory led to the end of the war. The Americans had won independence! Eight years later, it was time for the United States to elect its first president. Who was the country's first choice? George Washington, of course!

Battle Questions

Use the passage to answer the questions.

1. Which side was expected to win the War of Independence?

_____

2. Why?

_____

_____

_____

3. How did George Washington win the battle at Yorktown?

_____

_____

_____

4. Imagine that you could talk to George Washington after the battle. What questions would you ask him?

_____

_____

_____

_____

My Big Win

Write about a time when you had a big win or did something special. Maybe it was on the sports field or in the classroom or on stage or even at home. What did you do? How did you feel?

Draw a picture of your big win!

Painting from Bed
Frida Kahlo

As you read:

- Underline important words
- Circle confusing words or sentences
- Add drawings or notes to remember important facts

NOTES

_____

_____

_____

_____

_____

_____

_____

_____

_____

_____

Frida Kahlo grew up in Mexico. One day in 1925, she was in a terrible bus accident. She was only 18 years old. Her injuries were very bad. At first, no one knew if she would live. Frida had to stay in bed for months. Many of her bones were broken. She was in a lot of pain. But Frida was strong. And she was determined to get better.

Frida had been studying to be a doctor. She was smart and curious. She loved school. But her injuries meant she could no longer go to class. Frida was bored staying in bed. She borrowed her father's paints and paintbrushes. Frida's mother made her a special easel. It let Frida paint while she was lying on her back.

After creating many paintings from her bed, Frida realized that she didn't want to be a doctor. She wanted to be an artist.

Frida Kahlo succeeded. She became one of the most famous female artists of all time. The accident that caused Frida so much pain also inspired her. Painting helped Frida get through difficult times.

Describing Frida

An adjective describes a noun.
The adjectives below all describe Frida Kahlo.
Write each adjective in the correct sentence.

strong

curious

smart

famous

determined

Frida was very well-known. She was a _____ artist.

At school, Frida was a bright student and learned quickly.

She was _____.

She was eager to learn new things. She was always _____.

After her accident, Frida wouldn't give up. She was _____ to get better.

Frida wasn't weak-willed. She was a _____ person.

A Self-Portrait

Frida liked to paint pictures of herself. She never smiled in her self-portraits. Her face gives the paintings a serious feeling.

Draw a self-portrait.

What is your expression in your self-portrait?
What does your expression say about you?

_____

_____

_____

_____

_____

A Mystery Animal

Lewis Carroll was a writer. He once wrote about an animal with a big grin.
It could magically disappear. Sometimes when it disappeared,
the animal left its grin behind! What kind of animal was it?
Connect the dots to find out.

The animal was a _____ .

Lewis Carroll

Summer Movie Fun

Steven Spielberg is a film director. He directed the
first summer blockbuster. The movie was about
a scary animal. What animal was it?
Color the shapes that have a triangle
in them to find out.

Steven Spielberg

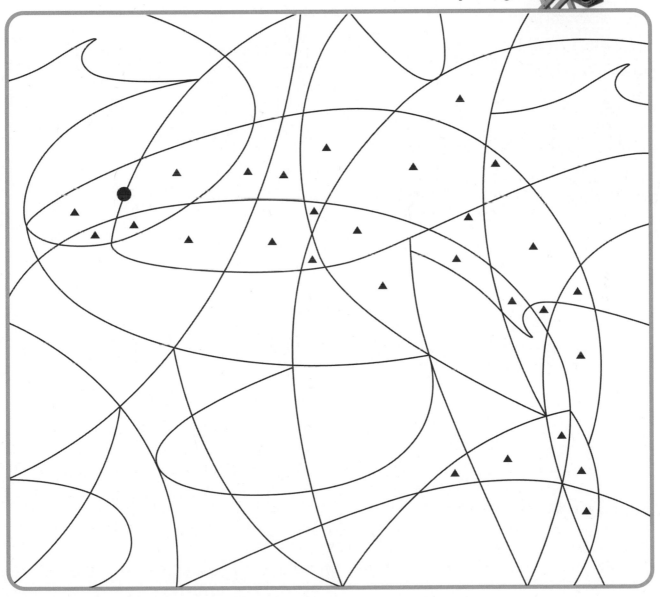

The animal was a _____ .

Believe It or Not!
Robert Ripley

As you read:

- Underline important words
- Circle confusing words or sentences
- Add drawings or notes to remember important facts

NOTES

_____

_____

_____

_____

_____

_____

_____

_____

Robert Ripley was a sports cartoonist. He drew pictures to go with sports stories in a newspaper. He drew cartoons of boxing matches. He drew cartoons of baseball games and golfers. One December afternoon in 1918, Ripley was in his office. He had no ideas for his next drawing.

Over the years, Ripley had collected weird and interesting facts. He kept a folder of these facts. He looked through the folder. He picked out some of those odd facts. Then he began to draw.

Soon, Ripley was finished. The drawing showed people doing amazing things. A man who walked backward across a continent. Another who hopped 100 yards in 11 seconds. A man who jumped rope 11,810 times in a row. He handed the drawing to his editor. Then he put on his coat and rushed out the door.

To his surprise, people liked the drawing. Ripley drew more of these weird cartoons. They became popular with readers. The cartoons were called *Believe It or Not!* Ten years later, Ripley's cartoons were seen in newspapers all over the United States. Robert Ripley showed everyone that the world was a marvelous place. It was full of extraordinary people. And they were doing extraordinary things.

NOTES

All About Words

Complete the word box.
For **Drawing**, draw a picture of something weird.
For **Examples**, write examples of things that are weird.
For **Nonexamples**, write examples of things that aren't weird—
things that are ordinary.

WEIRD

Definition in your own words	**Drawing**
_____ _____ _____	

Examples	**Nonexamples**
_____ _____ _____	_____ _____ _____

Synonym (word with the same meaning) _____

Antonym (word with the opposite meaning) _____

Related Words: Complete the word part to make a word with "weird."

_____ ness   _____ er   _____ est

I'm Special

What can you do that is special?
Write about a skill or talent that you have.

Believe it or not, I can _____.

_____

_____

_____

_____

_____

Draw a picture of yourself showing your special skill.

A Larger-than-Life King
Henry VIII

As you read:

- Underline important words
- Circle confusing words or sentences
- Add drawings or notes to remember important facts

NOTES

_____

_____

_____

_____

_____

_____

_____

_____

_____

Long ago, Henry VIII was the King of England. He ruled from 1509 to 1547. But when he was born, no one expected him to sit on the throne. His older brother, Arthur, was supposed to be king.

When Henry was 10, Arthur married Catherine of Aragon of Spain. But soon after he married, Arthur became sick and died. Suddenly, Henry was next in line to be King of England!

Then Henry's father died. Henry was only 17. A few weeks later, Henry married Catherine, his brother's widow. Some people thought it wasn't right for a widow to marry her dead husband's brother. But Henry didn't care. He loved Catherine.

Two weeks after his wedding, Henry was crowned King of England. At first, the people of England loved him. Henry was upbeat and bighearted. He especially liked to eat, drink, and throw big parties.

Henry allowed people in his kingdom to visit his castle. He listened to their stories of hardships and often agreed to help them. Sometimes Henry would free prisoners who had been thrown in jail unfairly.

But Henry went from being a generous and jolly king to becoming a mean and selfish ruler. Sometimes he was cruel, and he lost his temper quickly. Making him angry could cost you your life. Henry divorced Catherine and had five more wives. He even had some of his wives killed!

Henry was a king who will always be remembered—for good and for bad.

NOTES

A Royal Portrait

Write three interesting facts about Henry VIII.

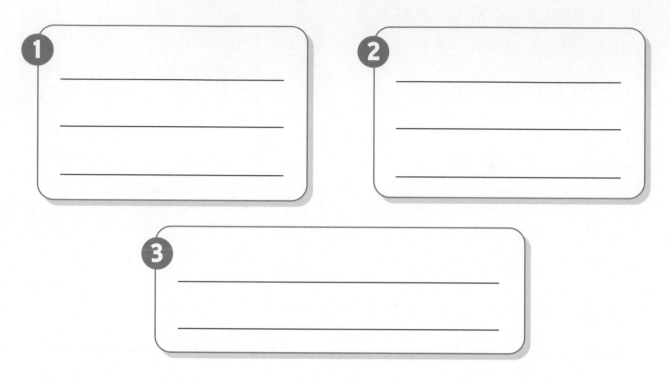

Draw a picture of one of your interesting facts about Henry VIII.

Good or Bad?

Henry VIII was a king who will always be remembered—for good and for bad. Write some reasons why this is true.

GOOD

_____

_____

_____

_____

BAD

_____

_____

_____

_____

A Trip Around the World
Nellie Bly

As you read:

- Underline important words
- Circle confusing words or sentences
- Add drawings or notes to remember important facts

NOTES

_____

_____

_____

_____

_____

_____

_____

_____

_____

It was January 25, 1890. A train rolled into Jersey City, New Jersey. Three timekeepers stopped their watches. Cannons fired. A large crowd applauded.

"Nellie Bly!" the crowd cheered.

A woman walked off the train. She tipped her hat to the crowd. Her fans cheered louder.

Nellie Bly had done it! She had traveled around the world. Her trip had taken 72 days, 6 hours, 11 minutes, and 14 seconds.

Nellie was a reporter. She worked for the _New York World_. It was one of the most famous newspapers in the United States. The newspaper had sent Nellie on her trip around the world. As she traveled, Nellie wrote about the countries she visited.

To keep readers interested, the *World* ran a contest. It asked readers to guess Nellie's return arrival time. The winner would get a trip to Europe. The *World* received almost a million entries!

Nellie's amazing race made her famous. Companies used Nellie's story to sell their products. There was a Nellie Bly board game, Nellie Bly trading cards, and even a Nellie Bly hat. The *New York World* sold more papers than ever before. It even published her life story.

Nellie Bly had become one of the best-known young women on Earth.

My Trip

Write about a trip you took. It could be a big trip.
Or it could be a little trip. Even a trip around the block can be
filled with adventure. It could even be an imaginary trip!

**What did you see on your trip?
Who did you meet? What did you do?**

_____
(title)

_____

_____

_____

_____

_____

_____

_____

_____

Write three words to describe your trip.

_____   _____   _____

Just the Facts

It's important for a reporter to get the facts right.
Read each sentence about Nellie Bly.
Write **true** or **false** on the line. Then write another true
sentence about Nellie Bly on the last lines.

Nellie Bly was a newspaper reporter for

the *New York World*. _____

Nellie Bly's trip around the world had taken over

75 days. _____

Her trip ended in Jersey City, New Jersey.

_____

The *New York World*'s contest asked readers to guess Nellie's

arrival time. _____

The winner would get a trip around the world.

_____

Write your own true sentence here:

_____

_____

_____

_____

_____

What's the Difference?

Jacques Cousteau was a famous ocean explorer. Look at the two pictures.
Can you spot 10 differences? Circle the differences.

Jacques Cousteau

The Game of Life
Milton Bradley

As you read:

- Underline important words
- Circle confusing words or sentences
- Add drawings or notes to remember important facts

NOTES

_____

_____

_____

_____

_____

_____

_____

_____

A young man stepped off a train in New York City. It was a September evening in 1860. Milton Bradley had come from Springfield, Massachusetts. Springfield was a big city. But it was nothing compared to New York. The streets were crowded. Everyone seemed to be in a hurry.

The women wore fancy hats with feathers. Their dresses were trimmed in lace. The men had tall hats. They wore suits with satin vests. Milton was impressed. But he hadn't come to New York City to admire clothes. He was there to convince people to buy and play a game he'd created.

The next morning, Milton took samples of his game and walked into a stationery store. The store sold paper, pencils, and pens. It also sold games and toys. Milton showed the store's manager his game. It was called The Checkered Game of Life. He explained how players moved across the checkered board. They made choices about life—both good and bad. The manager played the game with Milton. Then he bought all of Milton's sample games.

Milton brought samples to a different store. He sold them all of those samples, too. Milton was thrilled and proud. Over 150 years later, people are still playing The Game of Life. It is one of the most popular board games of all time.

NOTES

Opposites Attract

Draw a line to match the word on the left to its opposite.

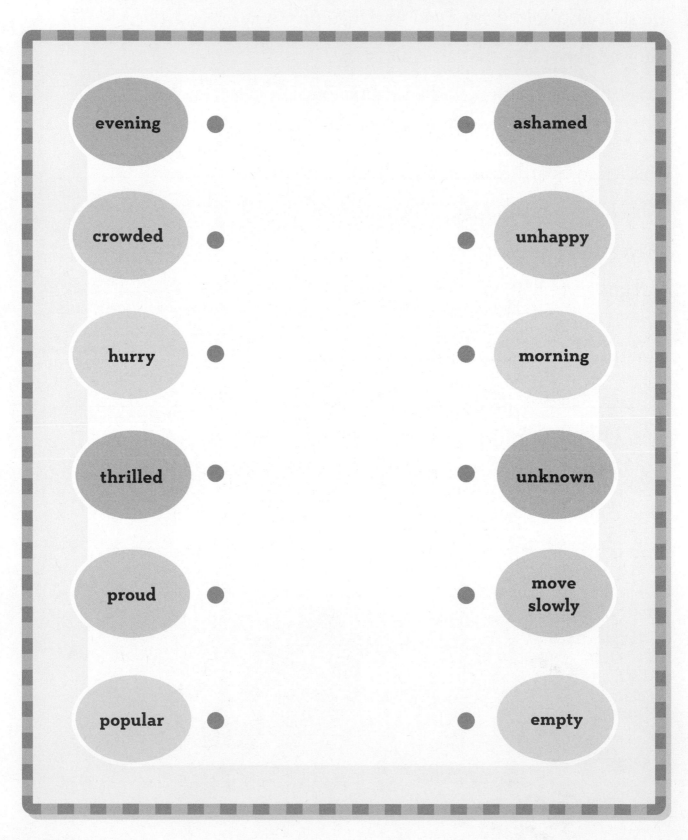

evening • • ashamed

crowded • • unhappy

hurry • • morning

thrilled • • unknown

proud • • move slowly

popular • • empty

Convince Me!

Milton Bradley went to New York City to convince people to buy his game. What is your favorite game? Convince a friend who never played it to give it a try.

My favorite game is

_____

I think you'd like it. Here's why.

Reason 1:

_____

_____

_____

Reason 2:

_____

_____

_____

Reason 3:

_____

_____

_____

A Love of Adventure
Jules Verne

As you read:

- Underline important words
- Circle confusing words or sentences
- Add drawings or notes to remember important facts

NOTES

_____

_____

_____

_____

_____

_____

_____

_____

_____

Jules Verne had always wanted to travel. He grew up on an island in France. As a boy, he had loved the ships that stopped there. He marveled at their tall masts. He had been amazed at the cargo they carried. The ships were filled with cocoa, spices, sugar, and fruit, such as mangoes.

Jules became a writer. He wrote poetry, plays, and magazine articles. But he wanted to write a book. He dreamed of writing an adventure story.

In 1859, Jules and a friend set sail from France. They were going to the islands of the United Kingdom. The pair sailed on a cargo ship. Jules was overjoyed. He stayed up at night to look at the stars. By day, he stood at the rail. He watched the ocean ahead for signs of land.

The two friends arrived in Liverpool, England. They took a train to Scotland. There, Jules was stunned. He admired the high mountains. He gazed at the rolling valleys and the misty lakes. On the way home, they visited the city of London, England.

After Jules returned to France, he started working on adventure novels. The books would make him one of the world's most popular authors. He took readers around the world on a series of marvelous adventures.

NOTES

Sailing Match-Up

Match each word and definition to its picture.

mast: a long pole on a ship that holds the sails •

•

cargo: the goods that a ship carries •

•

wheel: a disk that turns around a fixed, central point •

•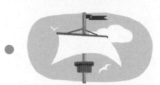

island: a piece of land that is entirely surrounded by water •

•

Write a definition for the word *adventure*. _____

_____

Draw a picture of yourself on an adventure.

Jules's Big Trip

Use the map and passage to answer the questions.

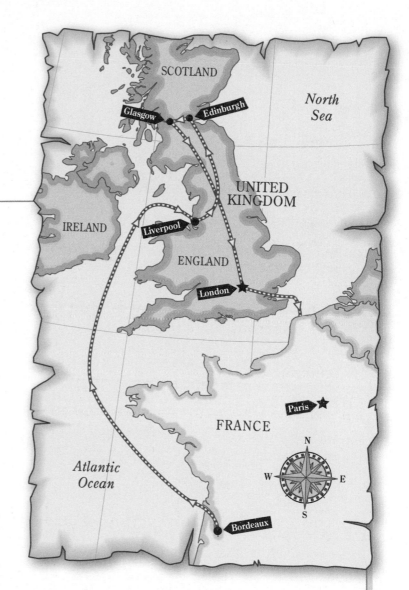

1. Draw a circle around Liverpool, England.

2. What ocean did Jules cross?

_____

3. How did Jules and his friend get from Liverpool to Scotland?

_____

_____

4. What did Jules see in Scotland?

_____

_____

5. What country is London in? _____

A Boy King
King Tut

As you read:
- Underline important words
- Circle confusing words or sentences
- Add drawings or notes to remember important facts

NOTES

_____

_____

_____

_____

_____

_____

_____

_____

_____

_____

Tut was born a prince. He spent his childhood in a palace in Egypt. Servants took care of him. Each day they brought him food. His servants also bathed and dressed him. They shaved his head. They left a braid of hair at the side. This was the hairstyle for a prince. While he slept, they fanned him with ostrich feather fans. That way, the heat would not disturb him.

When his father died, Tut became a pharaoh, or king. He was just a child. He was pharaoh for only about nine years. Tut died very young. He was just 18 or 19 years old. His mummy was buried in a secret tomb. There it stayed for more than 3,000 years.

But a man named Howard Carter searched for the tomb. He thought he knew where the king was buried. Finally, in 1922, he found it.

The discovery made headlines all over the world. Before this, nobody had ever heard of Tut. Suddenly, everyone knew his name. Today, King Tut is probably the most famous of all the pharaohs.

NOTES

Words from Egypt

Read the word in each pyramid.
Write a fact from the passage using each word.

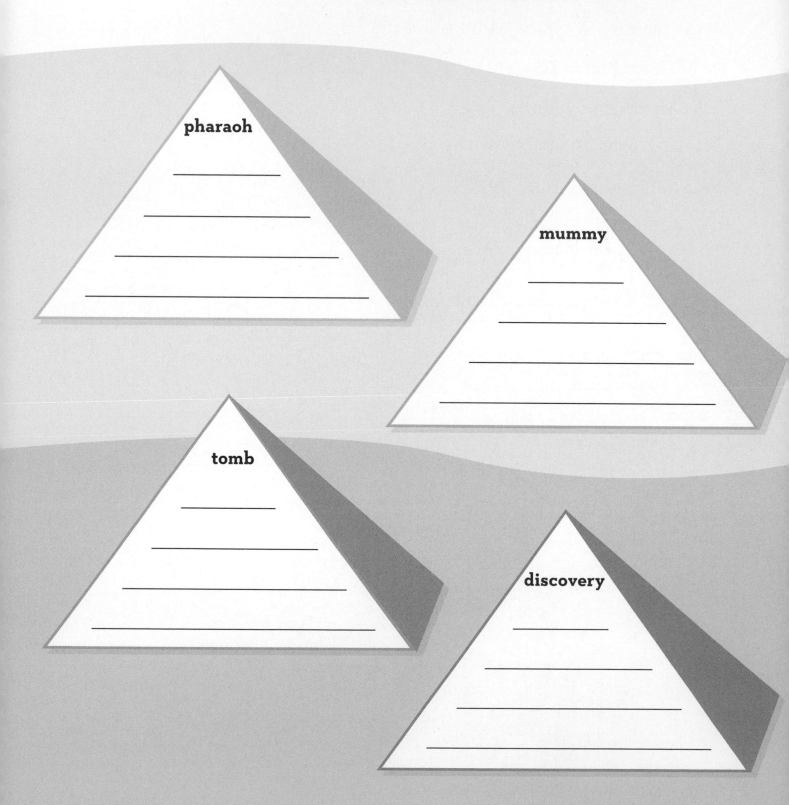

pharaoh

_____

_____

_____

_____

mummy

_____

_____

_____

tomb

_____

_____

_____

discovery

_____

_____

_____

_____

Prince Tut and Me

King Tut once was Prince Tut. How does your life compare to his? Fill in the charts and see.

Prince Tut

Where did Prince Tut live?

_____

_____

Who took care of Prince Tut?

_____

_____

How did Prince Tut wear his hair?

_____

_____

How did Prince Tut stay cool?

_____

_____

You
(draw yourself here)

Where do you live?

_____

_____

Who takes care of you?

_____

_____

How do you wear your hair?

_____

_____

How do you stay cool?

_____

_____

Around the Campfire

R. L. Stine writes scary stories. Make up your own scary story to tell around a campfire. Use the Idea Box to help you get started.

IDEA BOX

Character	Place	Time
scarecrow	amusement park	Halloween night
clown	cemetery	cold winter day
puppet	abandoned building	February 29
camper	cornfield	your birthday
you	campfire	warm summer night

R. L. Stine

Hats Off to Hats!

Davy Crockett was famous for his raccoon hat. What other hats can you find in the word search below?

RACCOON HAT	VISOR	BEANIE	HELMET
COWGIRL HAT	BOWLER	AVIATOR CAP	
BERET	BONNET	CROWN	

C	O	W	G	I	R	L	H	A	T
D	O	B	O	W	L	E	R	V	L
P	O	Y	R	I	U	E	R	I	S
R	A	C	C	O	O	N	H	A	T
O	L	E	P	T	H	N	H	T	B
B	E	A	N	I	E	V	E	O	O
E	E	R	E	T	A	I	L	R	N
R	C	R	O	W	N	S	M	C	N
E	D	M	T	R	C	O	E	A	E
T	A	T	K	R	N	R	T	P	T

Betsy Ross

Alexander the Great

Queen Elizabeth

Annie Oakley

Charlie Chaplin

Venus Williams

Amelia Earhart

Stand Up for Your Rights!
Ida B. Wells

As you read:

- Underline important words
- Circle confusing words or sentences
- Add drawings or notes to remember important facts

NOTES

_____

_____

_____

_____

_____

_____

_____

_____

In 1884, Ida B. Wells was a teacher. She lived in Memphis, Tennessee, and taught at a school nearby. She traveled by train to get there. Tennessee had a law stating that Black and white train passengers must ride in separate cars. Ida was a Black woman. She did not think the law was fair.

One day, Ida bought a first-class ticket. She rode in the ladies' car. It was only for white women. The conductor told Ida to move. She had to ride in the car for Black people. But Ida refused. The conductor and two other men dragged Ida out of her seat.

Ida fought back against the railroad.

She hired a lawyer and went to court. A judge decided that the railroad had been wrong. Ida was only twenty-one years old and five feet tall. But she had stood up to a powerful company and won.

Ida wrote about what had happened to her on the train. Her article was printed in a newspaper. It was very popular. Other newspapers across the country reprinted it. Ida became known as a brave journalist. For her whole life, Ida continued to work for the rights of Black people. She was brave and fearless. And she never backed down from a fight.

Ida B. Wells Wins Lawsuit!

Vocabulary Time

Choose the word from the word bank that completes each sentence.

Word Bank

journalist   popular   passengers   ignore   conductor   separate

1. When you _____ something, you don't pay any attention to it.

2. A _____ is someone who writes for newspapers.

3. If two train cars are _____, it means they are not connected.

4. _____ ride in cars, trains, buses, and airplanes.

5. Many trains have a _____ who collects the tickets.

6. Something that is _____ is liked by many people.

Not Fair!

Write about a rule that you think isn't fair. Tell why the rule isn't fair and why it should be changed.

_____

_____

_____

_____

_____

_____

_____

_____

_____

_____

_____

The Write Stuff **65**

A Fearsome Pirate
Blackbeard

As you read:

- Underline important words
- Circle confusing words or sentences
- Add drawings or notes to remember important facts

NOTES

_____

_____

_____

_____

_____

_____

_____

_____

_____

A pirate ship was lurking in the Atlantic Ocean. The year was 1717. Captains from the American colonies told stories about a pirate who was attacking their ships. He swooped in with his black flag flying. His men stormed the ships. They stole everything that wasn't nailed down.

The pirate captain had a long black beard. His beard covered most of his face. It had pieces of lit rope in it. The rope ringed his face in smoke. Pistols and swords hung from his belt. He was scary to look at.

The pirate continued his raids of terror. His ship sailed down the Atlantic coast

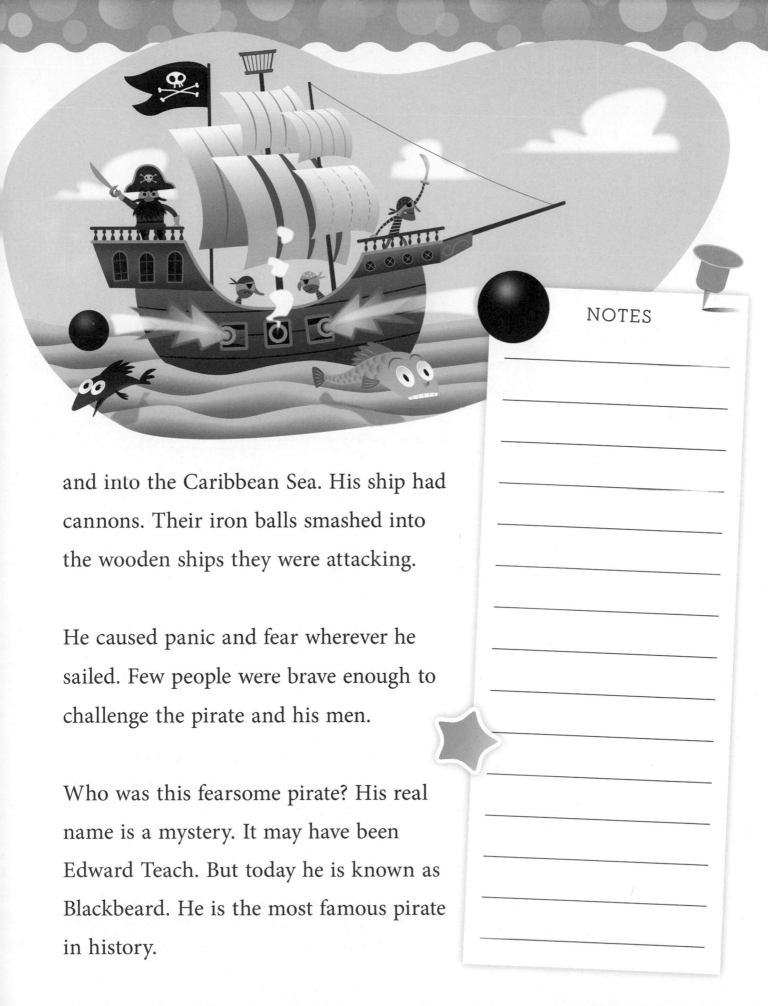

NOTES

and into the Caribbean Sea. His ship had cannons. Their iron balls smashed into the wooden ships they were attacking.

He caused panic and fear wherever he sailed. Few people were brave enough to challenge the pirate and his men.

Who was this fearsome pirate? His real name is a mystery. It may have been Edward Teach. But today he is known as Blackbeard. He is the most famous pirate in history.

A Picture of a Pirate

Write three interesting facts about Blackbeard
using details from the passage.

Draw a picture of yourself as a pirate. What are you wearing?
What weapons do you have?

Pirate Talk

For each sentence, circle the correct meaning
of the word in **bold** letters.

1. A pirate ship was **lurking** in the Atlantic Ocean.

   sailing   lying in wait   swimming

2. Their iron balls **smashed** into the wooden ships.

   bounced   banged   broke

3. The pirate continued his **raids** of terror.

   attacks   games   sounds

4. The rope **ringed** his face in smoke.

   rang out   circled   covered

5. Few people were brave enough to **challenge** the pirate and his men.

   arm wrestle   run from   stand up to

6. Who was this **fearsome** pirate?

   frightening   nervous   good-looking

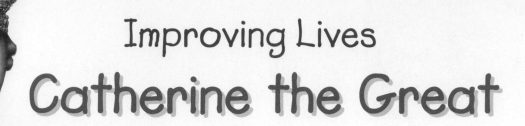

Improving Lives
Catherine the Great

As you read:

- Underline important words
- Circle confusing words or sentences
- Add drawings or notes to remember important facts

NOTES

_____

_____

_____

_____

_____

_____

_____

_____

_____

Catherine was an empress, or ruler, of Russia. She was made empress on September 22, 1762. On that important day, she sat on a diamond throne. She wore a silver dress trimmed with fur. Her crown had diamonds, pearls, and an enormous ruby. The crown weighed nine pounds.

Now that she was empress, Catherine was ready to act. Each day she woke up at six o'clock. Then she worked for fifteen hours. She studied everything she could about Russia.

Catherine wanted to improve the lives of ordinary people. And she did. She created many schools. A famous one was a school for girls. Catherine made many visits there. She even oversaw the lessons. Catherine built hospitals, too. Thanks to her, millions of Russians were protected against dangerous diseases. She also created a large museum called the Hermitage. It has one of the world's greatest collections of art.

Catherine ruled for 35 years. She is considered one of Russia's greatest leaders. Under her command, Russia became powerful. She earned her place in history. And she earned her name—Catherine the Great.

NOTES

The Hermitage

A Great Leader

Why was Catherine a great leader?
Write four facts that tell what she did for the people of Russia.

1

_____

_____

_____

2

_____

_____

_____

3

_____

_____

_____

4

_____

_____

You're in Charge!

Imagine you have just been crowned king or queen. Write about what you would do to make people's lives better.

In the White House

Read each clue. Then find the president's name and write it in the puzzle.

CLUES

Down

1. He was the first African American U.S. president.

2. This U.S. president wrote the book *Profiles in Courage*.

3. He was the only U.S. president elected four times.

4. This U.S. president wrote the Declaration of Independence.

6. This U.S. president had only one year of schooling.

Across

5. He was the first U.S. president.

7. This U.S. president starred in motion pictures and television shows.

John F.
Kennedy

George
Washington

Ronald
Reagan

Abraham
Lincoln

Barack
Obama

Thomas
Jefferson

Franklin
Roosevelt

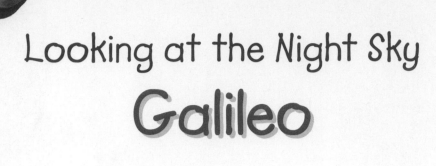

Looking at the Night Sky
Galileo

As you read:

- Underline important words
- Circle confusing words or sentences
- Add drawings or notes to remember important facts

NOTES

_____

_____

_____

_____

_____

_____

_____

_____

_____

_____

G alileo was a scientist. He lived in Italy. One night in 1609, he went outside. He carried a telescope. He had made it himself. His telescope could make objects that are far away look larger.

Galileo pointed the telescope at the moon. People living then thought that the moon was perfectly smooth. Galileo's telescope showed something very different. The surface of the moon was rough. It was filled with mountains, valleys, and craters.

One month later, Galileo made his greatest discovery. In January 1610, he aimed the telescope at Jupiter. He saw three bright bodies near the planet. What

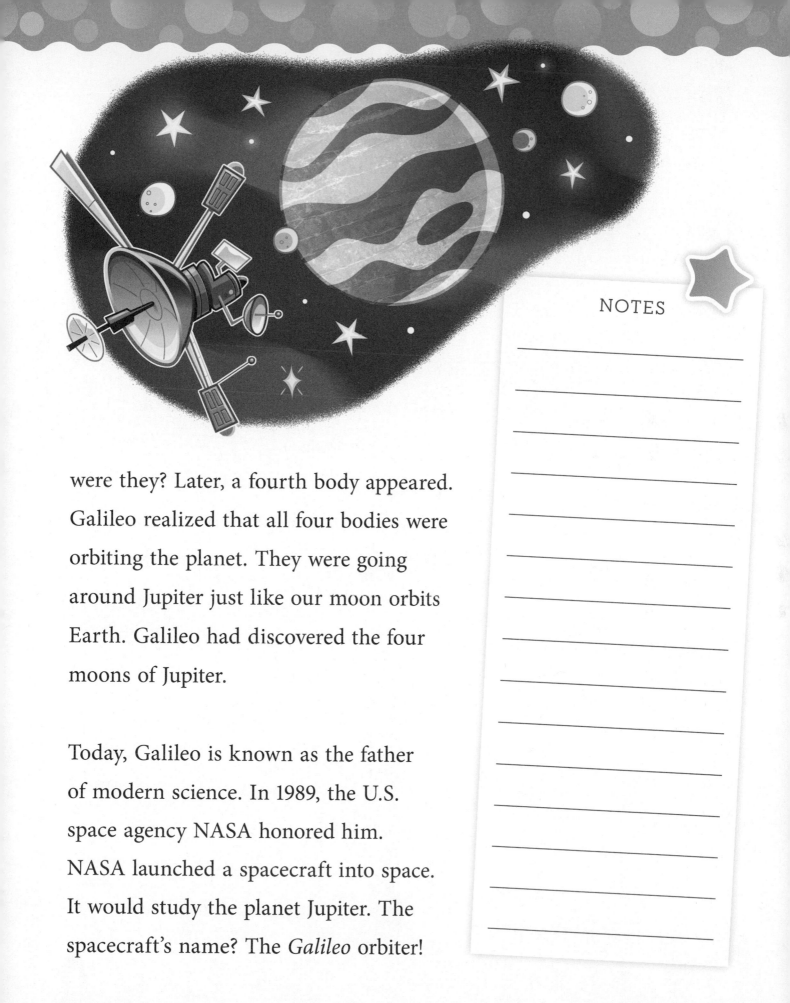

were they? Later, a fourth body appeared. Galileo realized that all four bodies were orbiting the planet. They were going around Jupiter just like our moon orbits Earth. Galileo had discovered the four moons of Jupiter.

Today, Galileo is known as the father of modern science. In 1989, the U.S. space agency NASA honored him. NASA launched a spacecraft into space. It would study the planet Jupiter. The spacecraft's name? The *Galileo* orbiter!

What Does It Mean?

Look at each word. Write a definition for the word. Use clues from the passage. Then write a sentence using the word.

telescope

Define: _____

_____

_____

Sentence: _____

_____

_____

enlarge

Define: _____

_____

_____

Sentence: _____

_____

_____

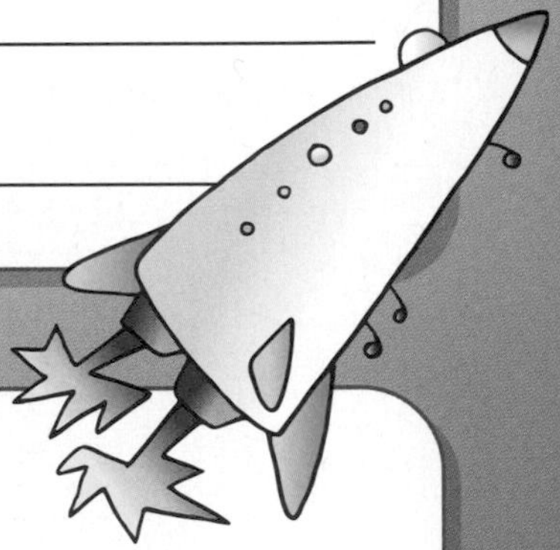

orbiting

Define: _____

_____

_____

Sentence: _____

_____

_____

launched

Define: _____

_____

_____

Sentence: _____

_____

_____

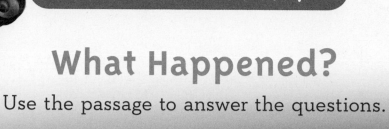

What Happened?

Use the passage to answer the questions.

1. What happened in 1609?

_____

_____

2. What happened in 1610?

_____

_____

3. What happened in 1989?

_____

_____

Choose one of the events. Draw a picture of it in the space below.

Martial-Arts Wiz
Bruce Lee

NOTES

_____
_____
_____
_____
_____
_____
_____
_____
_____
_____

In 1964, people were watching a young man. His name was Bruce Lee. Bruce was putting on a show in martial arts. The martial arts are ways of fitness, fighting, and self-defense.

First, Bruce did some push-ups. He did them with only one hand. Not only that, he did them using only two fingers of one hand. What strength Bruce had!

Then Bruce showed his "one-inch punch." A man stood in front of him. Bruce pulled his hand back just one inch. Then he thrust it forward with great force. The other man fell backward. What power Bruce had!

Finally, Bruce stood perfectly still. A man

stood in front of him. Suddenly, Bruce's hands flashed in the other man's face. Bruce didn't even touch the man. He was just showing how quick he could be. What speed Bruce had!

Bruce's amazing performance that day led to a new career. He was asked to try out for a part in a television series. He played the son of a fictional detective named Charlie Chan. The series never got made, and eventually the idea was canceled. But Bruce was a natural in front of the camera. Bruce later became an action-movie star. He used his martial-arts skills to fight the bad guys.

Bruce Lee died in 1973. But people still watch and enjoy his movies. He had it all—strength, power, and speed.

NOTES

Retelling Bruce Lee's Amazing Day

Fill in each blank to show what you learned about Bruce Lee.

1. To show how strong he was, Bruce

_____

_____.

2. To show how powerful he was, Bruce

_____

_____.

3. To show how fast he was, Bruce

_____

_____.

4. Because of his performance, Bruce was asked

_____

_____.

5. He became _____.

Today people still enjoy his movies.

POW!

POW!

How I Do It!

Think of something you can do well.
Describe how you do it to a friend.

How I _____

Step 1: _____

_____

Step 2: _____

_____

Step 3: _____

_____

Draw pictures that show each step.

Practice Makes Perfect
Duke Ellington

As you read:

- Underline important words
- Circle confusing words or sentences
- Add drawings or notes to remember important facts

NOTES

_____

_____

_____

_____

_____

_____

_____

_____

_____

It was the summer of 1913. Young Duke Ellington was on his way to Philadelphia. It was a trip that would change his life. Duke was going to Philadelphia to hear a piano player. Harvey Brooks played the piano in a new way. That way was called ragtime.

Duke had heard ragtime before. Almost everyone in America had. Ragtime was a popular musical style in the country that has a lively, bouncy rhythm. But the way Harvey played ragtime was different. Harvey's style was fast and flashy. His hands ran across the keys. It seemed as if his fingers never touched them. It was magic. Harvey had the attention of everyone in the crowd—including Duke.

Duke returned home to Washington, D.C. All he wanted to do was play piano like Harvey. He practiced day and night on his family's piano. He searched for ragtime piano players. Then he listened closely to them. He watched how they moved their arms when they played. Duke copied their style.

Duke watched and learned for many years. He became a piano master. He wrote his own music, too. He wrote over 3,000 songs. Duke Ellington was one of the greatest composers and musicians of the twentieth century.

NOTES

Musical Words

Look at the words below. Write a fact from
the passage using each word.

ragtime

_____

_____

_____

_____

keys

_____

_____

_____

_____

style

_____

_____

_____

composers

_____

_____

_____

A Fan Letter

Duke admired how Harvey Brooks played the piano. Write a letter to someone you admire. Tell the person what you like about them.

Dear _____,

_____

_____

_____

_____

_____

_____

_____

_____

Your friend,

_____

Plan a Garden!

Michelle Obama was the first African American First Lady of the United States. When she lived in the White House, she planted a garden. She grew spinach, tomatoes, berries, and many other good-tasting vegetables and fruit.

What vegetables and fruits would you plant? Use the space below to draw the plants you would grow in your garden.

Fairy Tale Mix-Up

The Brothers Grimm liked fairy tales—a lot!
The two brothers collected tales and put them
in books. What were some of these tales?
Unscramble the letters to find out.

D R E N I C L A E L

_ _ _ _ _ _ _ _ _ _

M O T   B U M T H

_ _ _   _ _ _ _ _

S P I N E G E L   T A U B E Y

_ _ _ _ _ _ _ _   _ _ _ _ _ _ _

T I T L E L   D R E

_ _ _ _ _ _ _   _ _ _

I I N D G R   D O H O

_ _ _ _ _ _   _ _ _ _ _

A-Mazing Soccer

Pelé is a world-famous soccer player from Brazil. He is known for his amazing kicks and goals. Help Pelé kick the soccer ball to the goal.

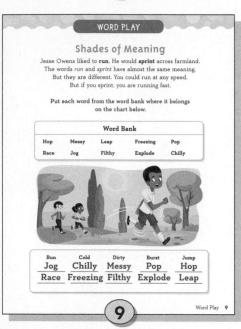

START

FINISH

4 Just for Fun!

4

Finger Puppet

The Muppets are famous puppets. But who made them? A man named Jim Henson did. His first Muppet was Kermit the Frog. Jim made Kermit out of an old coat, some cardboard, felt, and a Ping-Pong ball. Make your own puppet. Just follow the steps below.

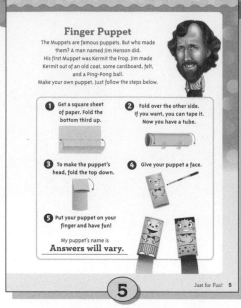

1. Get a square sheet of paper. Fold the bottom third up.
2. Fold over the other side. If you want, you can tape it. Now you have a tube.
3. To make the puppet's head, fold the top down.
4. Give your puppet a face.
5. Put your puppet on your finger and have fun!

My puppet's name is
Answers will vary.

Just for Fun! 5

5

Big News!

Jesse Owens won four Olympic gold medals. Reporters all over the world wrote about this important story. Imagine you were one of these reporters. Write your story about Jesse Owens in the space below. Make sure to answer the questions in the box.

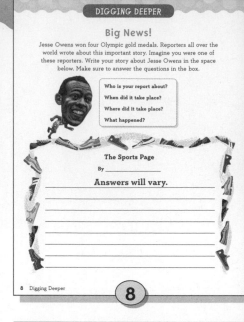

Who is your report about?
When did it take place?
Where did it take place?
What happened?

The Sports Page
By _____
Answers will vary.

8 Digging Deeper

8

Shades of Meaning

Jesse Owens liked to **run**. He would **sprint** across farmland. The words *run* and *sprint* have almost the same meaning. But they are different. You could run at any speed. But if you sprint, you are running fast.

Put each word from the word bank where it belongs on the chart below.

Word Bank

Hop	Messy	Leap	Freezing	Pop
Race	Jog	Filthy	Explode	Chilly

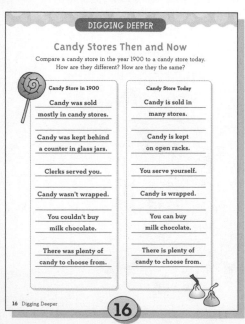

Run	Cold	Dirty	Burst	Jump
Jog	Chilly	Messy	Pop	Hop
Race	Freezing	Filthy	Explode	Leap

Word Play 9

9

Simile Match-Up

A simile compares one thing to another. Here are some examples:

In summer, the land was dry as dust. The girl's hair shone like a new penny.

Match the similes.

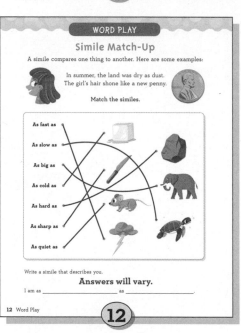

As fast as
As slow as
As big as
As cold as
As hard as
As sharp as
As quiet as

Write a simile that describes you.
Answers will vary.
I am as _____ as _____ .

12 Word Play

12

My Home

Laura's first book was called *Little House in the Big Woods*. Think about your home. Write a memory that happened there.

Answers will vary.

Draw a picture of your home.

Pictures will vary.

The Write Stuff 13

13

Candy Stores Then and Now

Compare a candy store in the year 1900 to a candy store today. How are they different? How are they the same?

Candy Store in 1900
- Candy was sold mostly in candy stores.
- Candy was kept behind a counter in glass jars.
- Clerks served you.
- Candy wasn't wrapped.
- You couldn't buy milk chocolate.
- There was plenty of candy to choose from.

Candy Store Today
- Candy is sold in many stores.
- Candy is kept on open racks.
- You serve yourself.
- Candy is wrapped.
- You can buy milk chocolate.
- There is plenty of candy to choose from.

16 Digging Deeper

16

My Candy Store

Milton Hershey was a candy maker. He also owned candy stores. Imagine you had your own candy store.

What is the name of your store? **Answers will vary.**
Where is your store? **Answers will vary.**
When is your store open? **Answers will vary.**
What candy is on the shelves? **Answers will vary.**
What do you do in your store? **Answers will vary.**

Draw a picture of your store.

Pictures will vary.

The Write Stuff 17

17

Hidden Chimps

Jane Goodall is a scientist who went to Africa to study wild chimps. Where are they? Find and circle all the chimps hiding in the picture.

Jane Goodall

18

How many chimps did you find? _____6_____

19

Baseball Talk

Look at the word in each baseball.
Write a fact from the passage using each word.

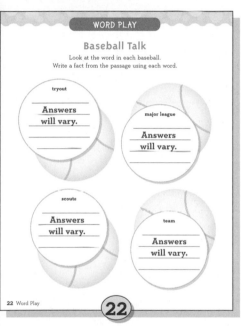

tryout
Answers will vary.

major league
Answers will vary.

scouts
Answers will vary.

team
Answers will vary.

22

Around the Bases

Answer each question to get around the bases.
Can you score a home run?

How fast did Roberto Clemente run the 60-yard dash?
In 6.4 seconds
Second Base

Which team did Roberto Clemente sign with?
The Brooklyn Dodgers
Third Base

What was Roberto Clemente's goal?
To be discovered by a scout from a Major League Baseball team
First Base

When was the tryout held?
On a sunny autumn day in 1952
Home Plate

23

Battle Questions

Use the passage to answer the questions.

1. Which side was expected to win the War of Independence?
The British

2. Why?
The British army was mighty and the world's best-trained fighting machine.

3. How did George Washington win the battle at Yorktown?
He sent his men to surround the British from all sides. The British army was outnumbered and trapped.

4. Imagine that you could talk to George Washington after the battle. What questions would you ask him?
Answers will vary.

26

My Big Win

Write about a time when you had a big win or did something special. Maybe it was on the sports field or in the classroom or on stage or even at home. What did you do? How did you feel?

Answers will vary.

Draw a picture of your big win!

Pictures will vary.

27

Describing Frida

An adjective describes a noun.
The adjectives below all describe Frida Kahlo.
Write each adjective in the correct sentence.

strong

curious

smart

famous

determined

Frida was very well-known. She was a _____**famous**_____ artist.

At school, Frida was a bright student and learned quickly.
She was _____**smart**_____

She was eager to learn new things. She was always _____**curious**_____

After her accident, Frida wouldn't give up. She was _____**determined**_____ to get better.

Frida wasn't weak-willed. She was a _____**strong**_____ person.

30

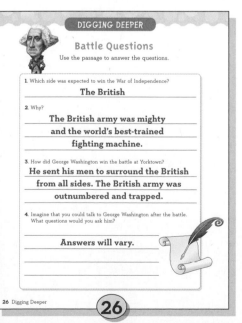

Answer Key **91**

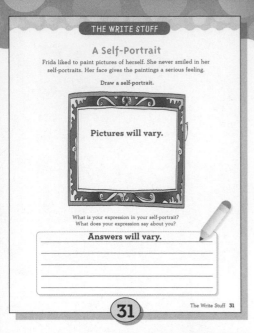

THE WRITE STUFF

A Self-Portrait

Frida liked to paint pictures of herself. She never smiled in her self-portraits. Her face gives the paintings a serious feeling.

Draw a self-portrait.

Pictures will vary.

What is your expression in your self-portrait?
What does your expression say about you?

Answers will vary.

The Write Stuff **31**

A Mystery Animal

Lewis Carroll was a writer. He once wrote about an animal with a big grin.
It could magically disappear. Sometimes when it disappeared,
the animal left its grin behind! What kind of animal was it?
Connect the dots to find out.

The animal was a _____ **cat** _____.

Lewis Carroll

32 Just for Fun!

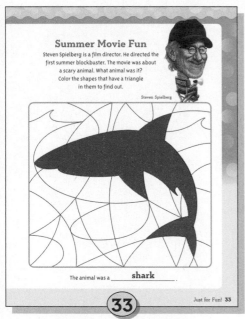

Summer Movie Fun

Steven Spielberg is a film director. He directed the first summer blockbuster. The movie was about a scary animal. What animal was it? Color the shapes that have a triangle in them to find out.

Steven Spielberg

The animal was a _____ **shark** _____.

Just for Fun! **33**

WORD PLAY

All About Words

Complete the word box.
For **Drawing**, draw a picture of something weird.
For **Examples**, write examples of things that are weird.
For **Nonexamples**, write examples of things that aren't weird—
things that are ordinary.

WEIRD

Definition in your own words	Drawing
odd or unusual	Pictures will vary.

Examples	Nonexamples
Answers will vary.	Answers will vary.

Synonym (word with the same meaning) **Answers will vary.**

Antonym (word with the opposite meaning) **Answers will vary.**

Related Words: Complete the word part to make a word with "weird."

weird ___ness   weird ___er   weird ___est

36 Word Play

THE WRITE STUFF

I'm Special

What can you do that is special?
Write about a skill or talent that you have.

Believe it or not, I can
Answers will vary.

Draw a picture of yourself showing your special skill.

Pictures will vary.

The Write Stuff **37**

DIGGING DEEPER

A Royal Portrait

Write three interesting facts about Henry VIII.

1 Answers will vary.

2 Answers will vary.

3 Answers will vary.

Draw a picture of one of your interesting facts about Henry VIII.

Pictures will vary.

40 Digging Deeper

THE WRITE STUFF

Good or Bad?

Henry VIII was a king who will always be remembered—for good and for bad. Write some reasons why this is true.

GOOD
Answers will vary.

BAD
Answers will vary.

The Write Stuff **41**

My Trip

Write about a trip you took. It could be a big trip.
Or it could be a little trip. Even a trip around the block can be
filled with adventure. It could even be an imaginary trip!

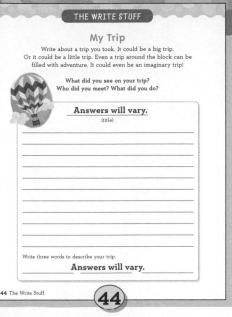

What did you see on your trip?
Who did you meet? What did you do?

Answers will vary.
(title)

_____
_____
_____
_____
_____
_____
_____
_____

Write three words to describe your trip.

Answers will vary.

44 The Write Stuff

44

Just the Facts

It's important for a reporter to get the facts right.
Read each sentence about Nellie Bly.
Write **true** or **false** on the line. Then write another true
sentence about Nellie Bly on the last lines.

Nellie Bly was a newspaper reporter for
the *New York World*. __**true**__

Nellie Bly's trip around the world had taken over
75 days. __**false**__

Her trip ended in Jersey City, New Jersey.
__**true**__

The *New York World*'s contest asked readers to guess Nellie's
arrival time. __**true**__

The winner would get a trip around the world.
__**false**__

Write your own true sentence here:
Answers will vary.
_____
_____
_____

Digging Deeper **45**

45

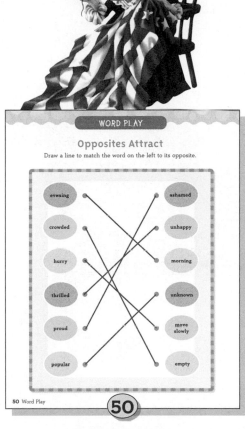

What's the Difference?

Jacques Cousteau was a famous ocean explorer. Look at the two pictures.
Can you spot 10 differences? Circle the differences.

46 Just for Fun!

46

Jacques Cousteau

Just for Fun! **47**

47

Opposites Attract

Draw a line to match the word on the left to its opposite.

evening	ashamed
crowded	unhappy
hurry	morning
thrilled	unknown
proud	move slowly
popular	empty

50 Word Play

50

Convince Me!

Milton Bradley went to New York City to convince
people to buy his game. What is your favorite game?
Convince a friend who never played it to give it a try.

My favorite game is
Answers will vary.

I think you'd like it. Here's why.

Reason 1:
Answers will vary.
_____
_____

Reason 2:
Answers will vary.
_____
_____

Reason 3:
Answers will vary.
_____
_____

The Write Stuff **51**

51

Sailing Match-Up

Match each word and definition to its picture.

mast: a long pole on a ship that holds
the sails

cargo: the goods that a ship carries

wheel: a disk that turns around a
fixed, central point

island: a piece of land that is entirely
surrounded by water

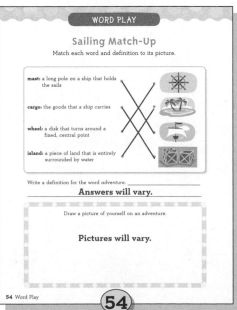

Write a definition for the word adventure. _____
Answers will vary.

Draw a picture of yourself on an adventure.

Pictures will vary.

54 Word Play

54

Answer Key **93**

DIGGING DEEPER

Jules's Big Trip

Use the map and passage to answer the questions.

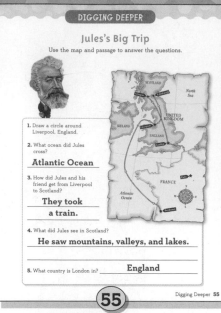

1. Draw a circle around Liverpool, England.

2. What ocean did Jules cross?
Atlantic Ocean

3. How did Jules and his friend get from Liverpool to Scotland?
They took a train.

4. What did Jules see in Scotland?
He saw mountains, valleys, and lakes.

5. What country is London in? **England**

WORD PLAY

Words from Egypt

Read the word in each pyramid.
Write a fact from the passage using each word.

pharaoh
Answers will vary.

mummy
Answers will vary.

tomb
Answers will vary.

discovery
Answers will vary.

DIGGING DEEPER

Prince Tut and Me

King Tut once was Prince Tut. How does your life compare to his? Fill in the charts and see.

Prince Tut	You (draw yourself here)
Where did Prince Tut live? **In a palace in Egypt**	Where do you live? **Answers will vary.**
Who took care of Prince Tut? **Servants**	Who takes care of you? **Answers will vary.**
How did Prince Tut wear his hair? **He had a shaved head with a braid at the side.**	How do you wear your hair? **Answers will vary.**
How did Prince Tut stay cool? **Servants fanned him with ostrich feather fans.**	How do you stay cool? **Answers will vary.**

JUST FOR FUN!

Around the Campfire

R. L. Stine writes scary stories. Make up your own scary story to tell around a campfire. Use the Idea Box to help you get started.

IDEA BOX

Character	Place	Time
scarecrow	amusement park	Halloween night
clown	cemetery	cold winter day
puppet	abandoned building	February 29
camper	cornfield	your birthday
you	campfire	warm summer night

Answers will vary.

R. L. Stine

Hats Off to Hats!

Davy Crockett was famous for his raccoon hat. What other hats can you find in the word search below?

RACCOON HAT   VISOR   BEANIE   HELMET
COWGIRL HAT   BOWLER   AVIATOR CAP
BERET   BONNET   CROWN

Betsy Ross
Charlie Chaplin
Alexander the Great
Venus Williams
Queen Elizabeth
Annie Oakley
Amelia Earhart

WORD PLAY

Vocabulary Time

Choose the word from the word bank that completes each sentence.

Word Bank

journalist   popular   passengers   ignore   conductor   separate

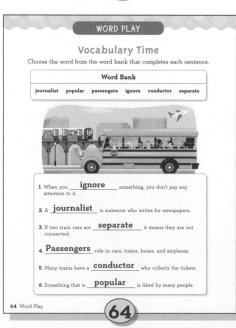

1. When you ___**ignore**___ something, you don't pay any attention to it.

2. A ___**journalist**___ is someone who writes for newspapers.

3. If two train cars are ___**separate**___ it means they are not connected.

4. ___**Passengers**___ ride in cars, trains, buses, and airplanes.

5. Many trains have a ___**conductor**___ who collects the tickets.

6. Something that is ___**popular**___ is liked by many people.

THE WRITE STUFF

Not Fair!

Write about a rule that you think isn't fair. Tell why the rule isn't fair and why it should be changed.

Answers will vary.

A Picture of a Pirate

Write three interesting facts about Blackbeard using details from the passage.

❶ Answers will vary.

❷ Answers will vary.

❸ Answers will vary.

Draw a picture of yourself as a pirate. What are you wearing? What weapons do you have?

Pictures will vary.

Pirate Talk

For each sentence, circle the correct meaning of the word in **bold** letters.

1. A pirate ship was **lurking** in the Atlantic Ocean.
   sailing — (lying in wait) — swimming

2. Their iron balls **smashed** into the wooden ships.
   bounced — banged — (broke)

3. The pirate continued his **raids** of terror.
   (attacks) — games — sounds

4. The rope **ringed** his face in smoke.
   rang out — (circled) — covered

5. Few people were brave enough to **challenge** the pirate and his men.
   arm wrestle — run from — (stand up to)

6. Who was this **fearsome** pirate?
   (frightening) — nervous — good-looking

A Great Leader

Why was Catherine a great leader? Write four facts that tell what she did for the people of Russia.

❶ She built hospitals.

❷ She created many schools.

❸ She made Russia powerful.

❹ She created a large museum for art.

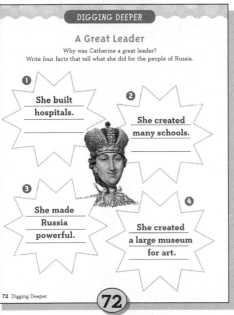

You're in Charge!

Imagine you have just been crowned king or queen. Write about what you would do to make people's lives better.

Answers will vary.

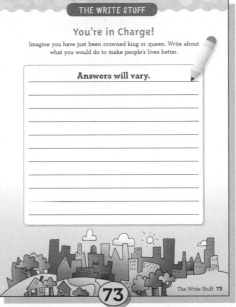

Crossword answers:
- BARACKOBAMA
- JOHNFKENNEDY
- FRANKLINROOSEVELT
- GEORGEWASHINGTON
- THOMASJEFFERSON
- ABRAHAMLINCOLN
- RONALDREAGAN

Abraham Lincoln
Barack Obama
Thomas Jefferson
Franklin Roosevelt

What Does It Mean?

Look at each word. Write a definition for the word. Use clues from the passage. Then write a sentence using the word.

telescope
Define: **an instrument used to see objects that are far away**
Sentence: **Answers will vary.**

enlarge
Define: **to make bigger**
Sentence: **Answers will vary.**

orbiting
Define: **traveling in a circular path**
Sentence: **Answers will vary.**

launched
Define: **sent into space**
Sentence: **Answers will vary.**

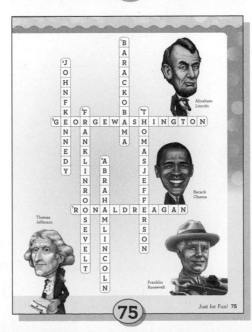

Answer Key **95**

What Happened?

Use the passage to answer the questions.

1. What happened in 1609?

Galileo used a telescope to look at the moon's surface.

2. What happened in 1610?

Galileo discovered the four moons of Jupiter.

3. What happened in 1989?

NASA launched the *Galileo* orbiter.

Choose one of the events. Draw a picture of it in the space below.

Pictures will vary.

79

Retelling Bruce Lee's Amazing Day

Fill in each blank to show what you learned about Bruce Lee.

1. To show how strong he was, Bruce

did some push-ups using only two fingers of one hand

2. To show how powerful he was, Bruce

showed his "one-inch punch"

3. To show how fast he was, Bruce

flashed his hands in a man's face without touching him

4. Because of his performance, Bruce was asked

to try out for a part in a television series

5. He became **an action-movie star**

Today people still enjoy his movies.

82

POW! POW!

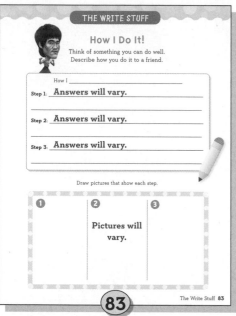

How I Do It!

Think of something you can do well. Describe how you do it to a friend.

How I _____

Step 1: **Answers will vary.**

Step 2: **Answers will vary.**

Step 3: **Answers will vary.**

Draw pictures that show each step.

① ② ③

Pictures will vary.

83

Musical Words

Look at the words below. Write a fact from the passage using each word.

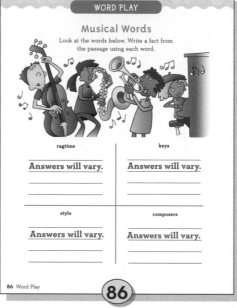

ragtime

Answers will vary.

keys

Answers will vary.

style

Answers will vary.

composers

Answers will vary.

86

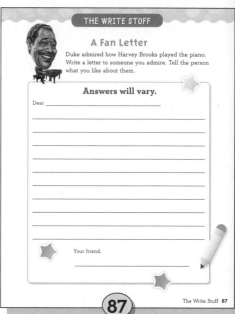

A Fan Letter

Duke admired how Harvey Brooks played the piano. Write a letter to someone you admire. Tell the person what you like about them.

Answers will vary.

Dear _____

Your friend,

_____

87

Plan a Garden!

Michelle Obama was the first African American First Lady of the United States. When she lived in the White House, she planted a garden. She grew spinach, tomatoes, berries, and many other good-tasting vegetables and fruit.

What vegetables and fruits would you plant? Use the space below to draw the plants you would grow in your garden.

Pictures will vary.

88

Fairy Tale Mix-Up

The Brothers Grimm liked fairy tales—a lot! The two brothers collected tales and put them in books. What were some of these tales? Unscramble the letters to find out.

DRENICLAEL
CINDERELLA

MOT BUMTH
TOM THUMB

SPINEGEL TAUBEY
SLEEPING BEAUTY

TITLEL DRE
LITTLE RED

IINDGR DOHO
RIDING HOOD

89